Partners in Practice

*Strategies for
Successful Peer Teaching*

by Susan Nelson

Fearon Teacher Aids
a division of
David S. Lake Publishers
Belmont, California

This book is dedicated to the children and parents of the Ramona Community School for having been my kind and patient teachers, and to the memory of Jesse Williams and John Coniff.

Illustrators: Marilynn Barr and Joe Shines

Copyright ® 1989 by David S. Lake Publishers, 500 Harbor Boulevard, Belmont, California 94002. All rights reserved. No part of this book may be reproduced by any means, transmitted, or translated into a machine language without written permission from the publisher.
ISBN 0-8224-5150-6

Printed in the United States of America

1. 9 8 7 6 5 4 3 2 1

Contents

	Introduction	iv
Chapter 1	To Teach Is to Learn Twice	1
Chapter 2	Organizing a Peer Teaching Program	7
	The Student-Organizer	8
	Working Partnerships	11
	The 100% Method	14
	Parallel Pairs	17
	Long-term Goals	19
Chapter 3	Using Games	21
	Basic Formats	23
	Board Games	25
	Concentration	29
	Dominoes	32
	Go Fish	36
	Turnover Games	37
	War	39
	Pocket Puzzles and Cover Boards	40
	Other Games	43
Chapter 4	Setting Up a Reading Program	49
Chapter 5	Motivation and Discipline	55

Introduction

I believe it was an eight-year-old girl named Abby who opened my eyes to the far-reaching possibilities offered by the use of peer teaching. Abby, at eight, was the oldest in a rather unusual elementary school class. The rest of the students ranged in age from 4½ to 7 and only one of them had been to school before. Abby had been to several schools and had learned to dislike nearly everything connected with school.

As the younger students in the class watched Abby tackle (and avoid) cursive writing, multiplication, geography, and other third grade subjects, both Abby and the subjects she studied became popular and interesting. This popularity and interest began to change Abby's perception of herself and, slowly, of her schoolwork. By the year's end, Abby was not only a more capable student and an invaluable tutor of the younger students, but also an eager learner.

In that classroom, peer teaching was not so much an idea or technique brought by me, but a natural occurrence. My only contribution was to allow it to happen.

Over the years I have come to believe that helpfulness and cooperation are natural to most people. It is only because we spend many years "unlearning" these virtues that competition supplants them so easily. This book describes how we might nurture a style of learning that will enrich a child's entire life.

Chapter 1

To Teach Is to Learn Twice

The large families of yesteryear are idealized by many writers and social scientists. The term "extended family" may bring to mind images and aromas of chicken and dumplings bubbling in a pot, Mother removing golden loaves of bread from a large cookstove, Aunt Sally in a rocker reading a story to a couple of children, older brothers outdoors chopping wood, and big sister tending a cooing infant. In this well-orchestrated group, everyone has a role and a set of tasks, and an impressive quantity of work is accomplished every day. An accurate historical picture? Probably not, but judging by how much some have mourned the loss of this fantasy family during the last twenty years or so, there may be something to learn from the structure of the extended family.

Today, families are smaller and most of the people who work with large groups of children are teachers. The modern classroom, however, is not structured like an extended family. Most of the children are the same age, are learning the same things, and are responsible for the same set of tasks. Or are they? A closer look reveals that, although children in the same grade are within a year or two of each other in terms of age, their maturity and skills vary widely. Goodlad and Anderson, in *The Nongraded Elementary School*, reported that ". . . in the average first grade there is a spread of four years in pupil readiness to learn as suggested by mental age data. As pupils progress through the grades, the span in readiness widens." A fifth grade teacher in a neighboring district reported to me a few years ago that students' reading levels ranged from second to tenth grade in her class. Teachers frequently view these wide ranges in ability as a dilemma, a giant hurdle to be ovecome. Might these differences instead be viewed as an advantage, or as a boon to effective teaching? My answer to this question is a definite yes.

Perhaps it would be a good idea to structure classrooms more like large families—that is, with a wide range in ages. Yet, the purpose of this book is not to propose large scale changes in the structure of schools. This book is meant to be used as a guide by any teacher in any elementary classroom. Although most teachers have little control over the ages of students in a typical single grade classroom, they can organize a family-like structure in the classroom by utilizing the wide range of abilities and maturity levels of their students. Social, emotional, and physical abilities should be considered along with academic ability. If two or three classroom teachers who use the methods described in this book decide that they can teach more effectively by "sharing" their students with each other, they can probably do so with a minimum of reorganization.

Jerome Bruner, in *The Process of Education*, has asserted that good instruction depends on economy of presentation. So it is with good ideas; if they are too complex, they are difficult to launch. This book presents some relatively simple ways for teachers to get their students to teach each other.

John Goodlad, author of *A Place Called School* reports, "One of the blind spots in American schooling is our almost complete failure to use peer teaching. In British schools you see children helping each other. The teacher has twenty-five assistants . . ." To fail to encourage students to help each other learn is a mistake. The benefits of doing so are enormous. Not only does learning take place more efficiently and thoroughly when peer teaching is used, but students experience cooperation and responsibility as an integral part of their education.

This collection of activities, games, and strategies has been compiled to enable the classroom teacher to individualize the teaching of basic skills by using every student in the class as someone else's tutor. The activities described here will keep students focused on the skills or facts to be learned. They are, for the most part, self-correcting; that is, they will allow students to work together with minimal supervision. They are also a vehicle for tapping the greatest human resource every school has in its possession—the students.

The Paideia Proposal by Mortimer Adler calls for a multifaceted approach to education. One of the three strategies Adler proposes for more effective education is "coaching," or small group teaching. This type of teaching gives students individual assistance with specific tasks. When working with a large number of students on skill areas, the teacher is usually presenting material that is too difficult for many students and too simple for others.

One of the ways teachers hope to do more small group teaching is to lobby for an increase in the size of the teaching staff in their schools. The likelihood of this increase seems to decline with each passing year. The learning tasks that this book addresses are not necessarily best taught by teachers or even teacher's assistants. Studying spelling words, memorizing math facts, or reviewing vocabulary words are simple, repetitive tasks. To insist that highly trained individuals directly supervise students while they practice these basic skills is like sending a tuna boat out to catch a minnow.

Certainly the teacher's organizational skills, creativity, and knowledge of curriculum are invaluable in designing and implementing a peer teaching program. During the early years, however, much of what students need to learn simply takes practice. Students who are relatively close in age and skill may be more willing to spend the countless hours helping each other practice new skills and less likely to grow tired and impatient than most adults. After all, peers have a better feeling for how difficult their learning tasks are, while adults, even experienced teachers and adoring parents, often find it exasperating that little Sara can't remember what $7 - 4$ equals, or can't differentiate between "where" and "were."

This isn't to say that children everywhere are innately inclined to spend their childhood years patiently helping their friends overcome academic difficulties. However, within a classroom or home arranged to encourage cooperation, most children do prefer working with each other to working alone in the same room.

Another way teachers have attempted to deal with students' individual needs is to rely more and more on homework and parents' help in monitoring homework. It is even common now to hear politicians and government officials in education calling for more homework as a means of upgrading public education.

Very early in the elementary grades, numerous notes go home with messages such as "Billy needs more practice with consonant sounds," or "Tammy could use more drill on her multiplication facts." Expecting parents to fit a lesson into what's left of the day after soccer practice, night school, piano lessons, gymnastics class, and Rotary Club meetings is a tall order. Moreover, late afternoons and evenings may not be the best times for youngsters to accomplish intellectual feats. Parents have a right to expect the school to make maximum use of what is undeniably the best part of the child's day. And a child has a right, after devoting six hours of the day to academic work, to pursue other interests, to play, or to relax.

The proposal that children help each other with their studies is not new, but it is not common practice in most of today's schools. Our present classrooms are usually structured in such a way that "Do your own work, please" is practically a classroom motto. Human beings are social animals; to work in solitude and relative silence while sharing close quarters with thirty or so peers is an unnatural phenomenon.

The ability to work independently is a desirable goal, but it is probably somewhat overrated in schools. In almost every other aspect of life, it is more important to be able to work with others than to work alone. The melding of ideas into a plan, the organization of a large group of people to accomplish a single goal, the ability to arrive at decisions acceptable to two people or a whole group—these are the qualities and skills which are of immeasurable value in business, science, government, and family life.

Independence can sometimes be stressed at the expense of learning. Very often, several or all of the students in a classroom are working on the same assignment at the same time. Reading and digesting information would be a more efficient and pleasant process if students worked in pairs or even small groups, helping each other locate key words and sharing information. However, this approach to studying is seldom used.

Alfie Kohn, in his compelling book *No Contest*, describes competition as a learned behavior. "That most of us consistently fail to consider the alternatives to competition is a testament to the effectiveness of our socialization. We have been trained not only to compete, but to believe in competition." Kohn argues persuasively that "superior performance not only does not *require* competition; it usually seems to require its absence." Teachers are unrivaled in their opportunity to demonstrate to the entire society the fruits of cooperation. Both intuition and research tell teachers that a student can frequently grasp material taught by another student more readily than when it is presented by the teacher. Part of this is because of the opportunity for a one-to-one experience and part because some students find it less anxiety-provoking to work with peers, especially when the material takes time to master.

In her autobiographical book *Blackberry Winter*, Margaret Mead attempts to define some of the circumstances of her childhood which led to her success as an adult. She recounts that in her home, which was also her school for a good portion of the time, children were treated more as people than as children. When children are given a chance to participate in the learning process as both teachers and students, they become more aware of what the learning process is about. They are given a chance at a role that elicits maturity.

Many people have observed how teaching can be a form of learning, but the French essayist Joseph Joubert (1754-1824) perhaps said it best: "Enseigner, c'est apprendre deux fois." (To teach is to learn twice.)

Chapter 2

Organizing a Peer Teaching Program

Several helpful strategies you might employ in organizing a peer teaching program are presented in this chapter. These procedures have been borrowed from nongraded programs, Montessori programs, and individualized programs, as well as from teachers in all kinds of settings. I have tried all the methods presented here and have found them useful.

Teachers who embrace the concept of peer teaching usually invent their own strategies for incorporating student teaching into their schedules, but the following recommendations may serve as a beginning. This chapter includes:

1. The Student-Organizer
2. Working Partnerships
3. The 100% Method
4. Parallel Pairs
5. Long-term Goals

In this book, I refer to the students as tutors and the classroom teacher as the teacher for the sake of clarity. In practice, I find it is more effective to call the student tutors "teachers" and refer to their help with other students as "teaching."

The Student-Organizer

A first step in creating a peer teaching program is to develop the students' organizational skills. It is much easier to monitor the progress of an organized worker than of someone who has only a fuzzy notion of what his or her responsibilities and accomplishments are. A student work log can aid students in getting a clearer overall picture of their assignments and responsibilities for a given period of time. It is my strong bias that the morning hours are the best time for strictly academic work, so the work period discussed here is an approximate two-hour block before the noon recess.

Sample Student Work Log

Name: Ginny
Date: 11/6/86
Oral Reading: Inside, Outside p. 43-48

Reading Workbook: Looking for Adventure p. 30, 31
Phonics: Book B p. 19, 20

Math: Plenty of Balloons p. 19 place value puzzle
Science/Social Studies: Rocks and Minerals p. 129-130
Teaching: (Tracy) Just in Time p. 15-19

On a log sheet such as this one, a student writes the title of the book he or she has worked in, and the pages completed on that date. The log might also include a listing for homework.

For the teacher, this log provides a way to check on student progress at a glance, but the real benefit is for the student. Because peer teaching depends to a large extent on different students carrying out different tasks at the same time, the log helps each student keep track of the assigned work. Students are allowed to budget their own time, choose the order in which to complete assignments, and decide when to complete their teaching duties.

If you have the freedom to individualize instruction, this type of assignment sheet makes it easy to do so. Students simply begin in their books each day at the place they left off the day before. After some initial consultation, students quickly develop a strong sense of what a standard assignment is, and you no longer have to make daily assignments for each subject. By doing a walk-around check on work logs, you can alert students to subjects which need correction or more work.

In a tutor/student partnership, the tutor decides when to work with the student. The tutor organizes the teaching materials, consults with the teacher if necessary, and notifies the student that it is time to meet.

The positive effects of these kinds of responsibilities cannot be overstated. When one walks into a room where students are checking their logs, glancing at the clock, selecting a book, and proceeding to work, all without direction from the teacher, there is a special atmosphere immediately apparent. Children, in general, enjoy each new freedom granted them. They take new responsibilities as a compliment, and their subsequent behavior reflects the dignity they feel. Another significant behavior found in classrooms where students are self-directed is the way in which students seek out the teacher for consultation, instead of waiting for the teacher to discover their errors or collect their work. Students also begin to seek help from their classmates, not only their permanently assigned tutors. When they do this, you are more available to answer the questions no one else can handle. You are then freed from answering questions such as,

"What's this word?" or "How do you spell _____ ?" These are the types of questions that can be answered by other students, and it does not take children long to figure out who can answer which questions.

You can enlist tutors to help younger students fill out their assignment sheets, and modify the work logs to meet the student's needs. Very young students who are given a choice of activities to complete in each subject area might be given a blank "ticket." You might tell students that they need to do, for example, a reading activity, a math activity, and a science activity during their work time. The student would bring you the ticket after completing an activity, and then you or a classroom helper would write down the activity and make a star next to it. A completed ticket might look something like this:

```
Name: Jeremy
Date: 11/4/86

Reading: ★
  Butterflies
    paper

Math: ★
  Workbook-
    p. 21

Science: ★
  Transportation
    puzzle
```

For older children who complete assignments that are longer and more involved, a work log can represent an entire week's work.

Example:

(front)

Week of _____		Name _____	
Subject:	Book/Project:	Monday	Tuesday
Reading			
Composition			
Math			
Science			
History			
Teaching			

(back)

Subject:	Wednesday	Thursday	Friday
Reading			
Composition			
Math			
Science			
History			
Teaching			

Working Partnerships

The permanent tutor/student pairs or groups represent the heart of the peer teaching program. As soon as you know your students reasonably well, you can make pair or group assignments. These pairs or groups are formed primarily for the purpose of oral reading.

As an example, suppose that your second grade class included students at the following reading levels:

Amanda 3.1	Joshua 1.5	Samantha 5.2
Barry 2.3	Katie 1.6	Travis 2.3
Chloe 2.5	Lana 2.5	Ulysses 2.6
Donald 2.8	Mercedes 2.7	Veronica 2.1
Emma 2.6	Namay 2.9	Wade 2.5
Francine 2.6	Orion 2.2	Yolanda 2.8
Galen 3.0	Patti 2.2	Zachary 2.9
Heather 1.9	Rusty 2.4	
Ian 4.5	Robert 3.3	

Obviously, reading levels should not be determined by any single test, but by a composite of tests, progress records, observation notes, and any other data which is available to the teacher.

You might form tutor/student partners as follows:

Tutor	*Student*
Orion (2.2)	Heather (1.9)
Patti (2.2)	Katie (1.6)
Veronica (2.1)	Joshua (1.5)
Donald (2.8)	Chloe (2.5) and Orion (2.2)
Yolanda (2.8)	Lana (2.5) and Patti (2.2)
Mercedes (2.7)	Wade (2.5) and Veronica (2.1)
Emma (2.6)	Rusty (2.4)
Francine (2.6)	Barry (2.3)
Ulysses (2.6)	Travis (2.3)
Robert (3.3)	Donald (2.8) and Yolanda (2.8)
Amanda (3.1)	Mercedes (2.7) and Namay (2.9)
Galen (3.0)	Emma (2.6)
Zachary (2.9)	Francine (2.6)
Namay (2.9)	Ulysses (2.6)
Ian (4.5)	Zachary (2.9) and Galen (3.0)
Samantha (5.2)	Amanda (3.1) and Robert (3.3)

A poster featuring names of partners can be displayed in the classroom for easy reference. Do not include the reading levels.

You might select suitable reading material for Ian (4.5) and Samantha (5.2), the most advanced readers, and let them read as partners or arrange to bring tutors for them from another class.

Students who do not have an opportunity to teach in this classroom might be enlisted to help in a first grade classroom. It is not necessary to place too much importance on the exact reading scores or levels. For the purposes of peer teaching, tutors need to be able to read slightly better than their students. You should inform the students that there may be changes within the first two weeks as an attempt is made to form the most workable partnerships. There is no denying that some students read better than others. To hide this fact would take massive manipulation on your part and would probably fail anyway. It helps to point out that while reading is important, it is not the only skill one possesses. It also depends somewhat on natural ability in the same way as does athletic prowess or artistic talent. Remind students that most people do not shine in all areas, and that a more able student should never belittle a less able student. The tutor's aim and responsibility are to try to share his or her talent and knowledge with others. Any tutor or teacher who simply points out what others do not know is not very useful. A teacher must find a way to impart knowledge and enhance the skills of others. Share your conviction with the students that if they help each other, everyone will learn more and learn faster. Teaching is as much a learning experience as being taught, sometimes more so.

Another type of tutor/student group that has met with success is a science and social studies reading group. For this type, you should group a relatively high level reader with a middle level reader and a low level reader. Make reading material in the science and social studies areas available. In this type of group, the highest level reader does most of the reading and is the official tutor; the middle level reader does a moderate amount of reading; and the low level reader reads only a few short passages, with help from the tutor as needed. You can make the same assignments for all three members of the group or make individual assignments. For example, the high level reader might formulate and answer questions about the material, the middle level reader might develop a vocabulary list with definitions from the material, and the low level reader might do an illustration with a short description related to the reading material.

The science/social studies reading groups have wide-ranging applications. They are a means by which students gain content information, additional oral reading practice, an opportunity to listen, and the experience of a close relationship with yet another group of students.

If you come to rely on peer teaching, you should know at all times which concepts your students have mastered in order to understand how each student can be of help to someone else. If both you and your students know what work has been completed, all parties will have a much better idea of the kinds of help that can be offered, and by whom.

One practical means of assessing progress quickly and accurately is to require students to complete all assignments. In this case, completion does not simply mean answering all the questions in an assignment or writing a paper, but answering all the questions correctly and rewriting a paper until it is as polished as possible.

Many teachers who insist that students correct most of their work are considered unrelenting perfectionists. If students of any age are accustomed to settling for inaccurate, haphazardly completed assignments, they may initially resist such thorough scrutiny of their work. In the final analysis, however, the teacher who is a bit of a perfectionist is probably attuned to the *desire* of young children to stand on their tiptoes when it comes to matters of achievement. In *Childhood and Society*, psychologist Erik Erikson describes the elementary school child as being immersed in a period of psychological development he calls "industry versus inferiority." This is the stage during which skill acquisition, productivity, and completion are paramount in the child's life. Other psychologists refer to the aim of maximizing one's potential as "self-actualization." Whatever the terminology used, it becomes clear that mediocrity is associated with feelings of inadequacy and inferiority. Erikson also cautions that an overemphasis on outcomes without sufficient attention to the *process* of achievement can foster conformist tendencies and exploitive behavior. Peer teaching provides an ideal situation for demonstrating to students the importance of cooperation and helpfulness, and an opportunity for students to develop healthy attitudes about working with others of both greater and lesser ability.

A positive side effect of peer teaching is that students will develop a sense of how to evaluate their own success. Casting each student in a teaching role is an effective way to point out that the classroom teacher is not the only one with the ability to make judgments. Furthermore, students come to appreciate the teacher's answers and advice as they struggle to make accurate assignments and find that this involves gathering and synthesizing all the available data.

Suppose that a student reads a chapter in a science textbook and answers the questions at the end, but gets ten of thirty items wrong. It is not safe to assume that the student understood that material well enough to help another student comprehend that same material. If this student goes back and rereads portions of the text and corrects those ten wrong answers, however, he or she has completed the work with 100% accuracy. You can now assume that the student has derived some basic understanding of the chapter.

The same is true for a page or even a whole chapter of mathematical operations. If a student does forty long division problems and makes five or ten errors, you might assume that the student is familiar with the basic concepts of long division. Not until those five or ten problems have been examined, though, do you know what else the student needs to learn about long division. Random calculation errors are a signal that perhaps fewer problems should be assigned, with a greater emphasis on accuracy.

In math especially, teachers tend to assign large quantities of work without ensuring that students will be able to find and correct errors as they proceed. This is a counterproductive way to learn a skill. One doesn't need to continually repeat a process one has already mastered, and it is useless and perhaps harmful to repeat a process incorrectly. (A good computer program that teaches mathematical operations often solves these problems.)

If a student makes errors because he or she used faulty processes, both you and the student need to know this. The difficulties the student had with these problems must be overcome. After the problems are dealt with and corrected by the student, you can assume that the student can do the work involved and will also be able to help another student with that same material.

Students who are taught to concentrate on accuracy and quality rather than quantity learn to be dissatisfied with incomplete or inaccurate work. Such students also develop good judgment about when to seek assistance. They internalize high standards for themselves and their peers.

A final note about completing work with 100% accuracy—if a student is asked to rework assignments and correct errors and still must take home a paper with red marks and scrawls all over it and a large -9 at the top, it will hardly seem worth the effort from the student's perspective. If students are asked to do their work in pencil and you make corrections in pencil, the student has a chance of creating a final draft of which he or she can be proud.

There are many popular reasons for using all that ink on student papers, but no matter how plausible the reasons, the end result is still the same—a vandalized paper that sometimes has more teacher writing than student writing on it. If one argues that this is making a fuss over nothing, the implication is that these papers are not very important. On the contrary, in the world of school, papers and workbooks are very important.

Students are among the few groups of people who are not given a chance to correct their errors and make their work look good. Architects and lawyers are not required to show their clients initial sketches and rough drafts. Clothing designers do not include, in their fashion shows, items that were sewn wrong side out. One reason many of us expend so much effort in our various professions is that we like to have an impressive product to display. In school, the only child who ends up with impressive-looking papers is one who did not make any errors the first time around. In real life we all make errors, and admitting and correcting them is part of intelligent living.

There are many devices you can use to help students end up with polished papers. Paperclips, stick-on notes, and removable tape can aid in this process. You can circle misspelled words, for example, and write the correct spellings in the margins. When the student has made the corrections, he or she can erase the circles and margin notes. Whatever methods you use, the goal is to avoid penalizing students for needing a practice run or first draft. Students are better able to keep in mind the true objectives of their schooling if what they produce is treated as *real* work.

Parallel Pairs

Perhaps one reason teachers shy away from such a strong emphasis on accuracy is that they fear that checking and reworking and checking again will slow progress down to a snail's pace; not enough material will be covered. With peer teaching, the rate at which students can complete assignments can be significantly increased. In addition, students who learn material well, who take the time to understand what they are doing rather than just get through it, make fewer errors as time goes by, have less difficulty with their assignments, and produce work of ever increasing quality. Why? All learning builds on previous learning. If the previous learning has taken root, future learning will be greatly enhanced.

Rather than insisting that students read chapters and answer questions independently, teachers can have students work in pairs. Two students can read the material aloud to each other or read on their own and then join forces to review the questions and problems together. The old saying "two heads are better than one" is very apt in this situation. Whenever a person of any age reads a book or an article and rereads it again at a later date, he or she discovers how much new information can be gleaned the second time around. If two students read the same material and look at a set of questions about that material, it is inevitable that certain information that was missed by one of them will be noticed by the other, and vice versa. There is no reason that students should not share their perceptions and strengths. Much evidence suggests that a combination of visual and auditory learning is superior to the exclusive use of one or the other. In this situation, students are given the opportunity to review the text as well as discuss their findings with their partner.

Partnerships for the purpose of studying together in this way may be formed casually rather than assigned, and may last a couple of hours, days, or weeks, depending on the assignment. The partners are "parallel" in that they are both working on the same or a similar assignment. They need not be perfectly matched for ability, and there is no need to designate one as tutor and one as student.

Some teachers may fear that student partnerships of this kind will result in one partner doing all the work while the other remains passive and fails to make a contribution. If this were to occur, it would correct itself shortly. First, both students realize that it is a waste of time to rely on the efforts of only one of them. Second, the producing partner would not stand for the inequity for very long. If no other solution could be arrived at, the "worker" would probably start giving the "nonworker" assignments. He or she might say, "If you're just going to sit there, look up these words," or "Why don't you reread the introduction to see if we can find the answer to this question?"

It is important for the teacher to structure the schedule so that wasting time is not rewarded. It is possible to arrange a day, a week, or even an hour so that the emphasis is on accomplishing a certain task or set of tasks and not simply on keeping a low profile. A hurried teacher often appreciates the student who doesn't make demands, yet the student may perceive the teacher's message as, "I will excuse you from this work period (assignment) if you appear to be working hard and keep relatively quiet for now. I appreciate your *effort*." The student's "effort" however, may consist of staying out of the way and wasting time rather than actually working. In order for students to learn, they will need help. Teachers can be overwhelmed by the amount of help needed by so many students.

Another message perceived by students is, "Smart students work independently and don't need much of my help." Unfortunately the very young hear this message most loudly. At an age when learning and growing are the most important elements in a child's life, he or she will make every effort to be perceived by others as a competent being. But avoiding assistance can be an intellectual disaster for many young children. Making it normal for students to enlist each other's help goes a long way toward solving this problem. It also sets up a valuable and self-perpetuating tradition of giving and receiving that is likely to permeate every aspect of a child's life.

Long-term Goals

As much as possible, let students know the long-term objectives of their day-to-day work. Students are eager to hear about what they will be able to do in six weeks or at the year's end. If students are kept abreast of where they are headed academically, they are more likely to participate in moving toward those goals.

One of the most frustrating aspects of my student teaching days was the fact that I felt that I was always "waiting for orders." This is not a manner in which I am accustomed to working, but in this classroom, as in many, the only person who seemed to know which activity followed the present one was the teacher. Even in a kindergarten class, children will respond positively to information such as, "By winter break, most of you will know the sounds of all of the letters of the alphabet. We will be able to count to fifty as a group, and we will learn several new songs and poems for our winter pageant."

The idea is to inform and thereby enlist the students' cooperation. Certain students, when they comprehend the long-term goals, will take the initiative to do extra work in order to arrive at those goals early. In a peer teaching program, this means that you will have some very able assistants in a short time.

If you plan a unit on geography in which several countries or continents are going to be studied, let students know at the outset what will be covered and to what extent. Sometimes the cheers or groans that accompany the presentation of such an outline can help the teacher decide which parts of a unit need some spice.

In most college courses, students are presented with a syllabus because it is assumed that students will handle the same work in different ways. The syllabus allows students to take the initiative in scheduling their study time and completing assignments. The same initiative can be encouraged in very young students.

Anyone who has ever been on a car trip with youngsters can attest to the fact they they are *very* interested in where they are going and when they will arrive. If this same intense curiosity is not apparent in their academic excursions, it is quite possible that children are not aware of the road on which they are traveling. It is difficult, even frightening, to imagine moving forward when you have no idea where you're headed.

Along with the expected pleasures and status of advancing to the next grade, students can be taught to look forward to what they will *do* when they get there. They may enjoy being able to state, "Next year I will learn to write in cursive," or "This fall I will be learning about ancient civilizations," or "In a few weeks I'm going to learn to add and subtract fractions."

Chapter 3
Using Games

Most teachers interested in bringing variety to their classrooms and encouraging active participation by students have probably sifted through countless idea books about games and activities. Two stumbling blocks that keep teachers from putting the ideas to work are:

1. Mechanical problems—The activity is difficult to make. Materials are expensive or difficult to obtain. The items are hard to store and keep track of.

2. Operational problems—Once the game is constructed, the return on the investment is poor. Too much time is wasted learning rules (student's time) and supervising play (teacher's time), and too little relevant learning takes place.

This chapter is written to help you utilize learning games and make the most of both your and the students' time and energy. If students are going to work with each other productively, they need to spend a maximum of time on task, allowing you the opportunity to observe and evaluate their progress literally at a glance.

Games can work well for peer teaching for several reasons:

- Many of the skills elementary students must learn require drill and practice.
- Games hold most students' interest better than fill-in-the-blank and worksheet assignments.
- Elementary age students are inclined to play in pairs or small groups. Drilling on rules of phonics with a friend is a far more attractive proposition than completing a workbook assignment. Many teachers complain that students talk in class, but the wise teacher integrates the talking, making it a part of the required work and thereby decreasing discipline problems that involve talking.
- While some students are able to absorb basic skills through pencil and paper activities, many students are not. These students rely much more on oral transmissions of information. Because you cannot speak to each child individually all day long, games can provide one way for children to get the oral practice and auditory feedback they need.

To get the most mileage (learning) out of peer teaching with games, the first ground rule for teachers is to *standardize the games for classroom use.* Most of the games described in this book are not new or original. On the contrary, they are the games most children and adults are already familiar with. Yet, adapted for learning purposes, these games become valuable teaching tools.

If students spend a large share of their time and energy struggling with rules and directions and haggling over points earned, games will not be efficient learning tools. You should select a few simple games, teach them to the students, and then adapt the various skills to these few game formats. In this way, the games become second nature to the students and the students can give their concentration and effort to the subject matter presented. Once students have a basic repertoire of well-known games, new formats can be added one at a time.

The second ground rule for effective use of games is to *avoid using games as a reward.* Playing "Rhyming Dominoes," for instance, should not be a reward for completing phonics worksheets about rhyming, but instead a substitution for the worksheets. When cooperative learning becomes commonplace, it is easier to monitor. If games are used as rewards instead of as assignments, students will see them as playtime activities. When the morning math assignment is fifteen to twenty minutes of "Multiplication War," the students understand that this is their work and they take it seriously. Because students complete oral activities more rapidly than written assignments, more drills can be covered in a shorter time.

The third ground rule: *keep it simple.* Complex rules and game strategies are challenging in and of themselves and can interfere with the primary aim of the learning. Avoid such game instructions as "miss a turn," "go back two spaces," "take an extra point," and so on. Strip the games to their basic structures so that a minimum of effort is needed to learn, play, and supervise the game. As mentioned above, the students should give their effort to learning skills. The win-or-lose aspect of games can be diminished by having students play for a set length of time, or play until both players reach a given point. The game merely provides a framework for practicing skills.

The general goals are for games to become as commonplace as worksheets, and for children to become used to helping each other. Peer teaching through games will not replace written work, but when incorporated into the classroom routine, it becomes an invaluable addition to the teacher's arena of expertise.

Basic Formats

There are seven basic formats for games presented in this chapter. They are:

1. Board Games
2. Concentration
3. Dominoes
4. Go Fish
5. Turnover Games
6. War
7. Pocket Puzzles and Cover Boards

Most of the skill games involve some kind of matching process. In order to practice addition, a student matches *3 + 2* with *5*. To practice phonics skills, a student might match "phone" with "groan" (rhyming) or "<u>ph</u>one" with "<u>f</u>ull" (consonant digraphs). To practice telling time, he or she might match *12:45* with a picture of a clock depicting *12:45*.

Some games require students to correct each other. For these games, it is helpful if one player has slightly better skills than the other(s). However, this is not absolutely necessary. Even when two students are fairly close in skill level, chances are good that there are wide variations in their knowledge of specific facts. Because no two minds work exactly alike, two students who work together can share their knowledge and end up with a more complete understanding of the material.

Once you and your students have a repertoire of games, there is virtually no limit to their applications. History, science, and geography facts, as well as spelling, math, and phonics problems can be put on cards and reviewed by students. The opportunity to practice reciting facts also helps fulfill the general knowledge requirements of the elementary curriculum.

Some sample lists and games are presented in this chapter to give you some ideas about how the games can be used. Other games can be developed to include specific facts or skills that need review or reinforcement in a particular classroom. One good source of lists for making games is *The New Reading Teacher's Book of Lists* by Fry, Fountoukidis, and Polk (Prentice-Hall, 1985). The best reference for the content of learning games, of course, is the work that is going on in the classroom. Whether a class is studying astronomy, reptiles, simple addition, or parts of speech, there are basic facts which can be translated into game format for independent review by students.

Perhaps it is somewhat inaccurate to describe the activities in this book as games. In truth, they might be considered worksheets with moveable parts. The success that results from using these game formats for study can be attributed not so much to their amusement value, but to the fact that they encourage students to help each other.

Construction

Nearly all of the games and activities presented in this book can be made quickly and easily with relatively inexpensive materials. Index cards of various sizes and colors can be used for most of the card games. You can collect dice and markers from a variety of sources, make gameboards from posterboard or colored file folders, and draw or cut pictures and decorations out of discarded workbooks.

Storage

Store materials in a practical way, such as on open shelves and in open containers. This makes it easy to do a walk-around check to see that everything is in its place before students go home or out to play.

Board Games

The basic game board has a starting place, a finishing place, and thirty or forty spaces in between. Game boards are usually used with cards, markers, and dice or spinners. Make cards for board games complete with answers so that students can play independently. Opponents can pick up the cards and read the questions.

A simple version of a game board has colored circles with a connecting line. Such a board might be decorated with pictures of sea life, animals, cars, or any number of things that children love.

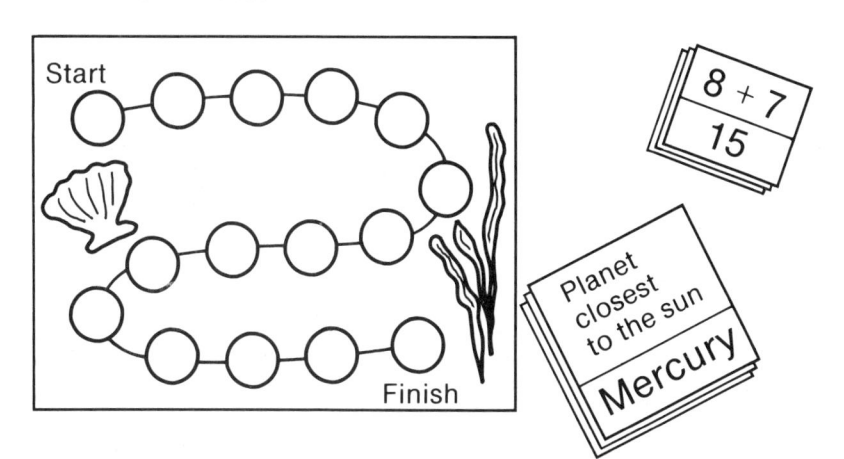

Baseball Game Board

This board uses four sets of cards with ascending levels of difficulty. Players use a marker to "run" around the bases and can choose whether to try for a single, double, triple, or home run. Players read questions to each other.

This is a good game for reviewing spelling words. Weekly list words could be used as follows:

Review words—Single
Last week's words—Double
This week's words—Triple
Next week's words—Home run

Write the values in pencil so they can be changed. Use *S*, *D*, *T*, and *H*.

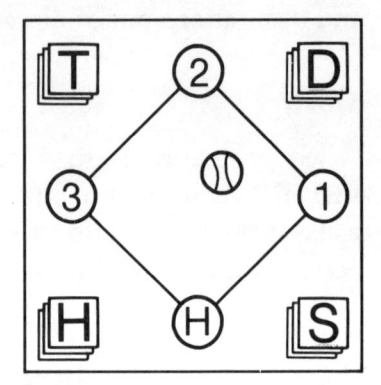

Tug of War

This is a good board to decorate with a jungle motif as in the African folktale "Tug of War."

Make a board with a slightly larger space in the middle and three evenly spaced parallel lines on either side. A long string with a button or bead tied at the center serves as the marker. Each time a player gets a correct answer he or she pulls the button over one line toward his or her side. The winner is the first player to pull the bead into the last space on his or her side.

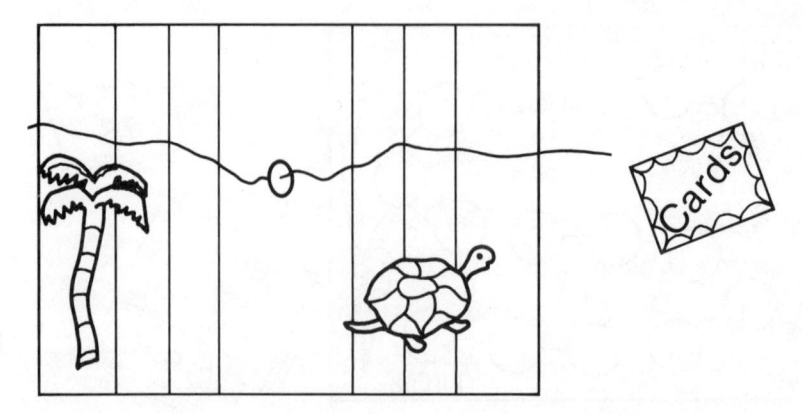

Football Board

The football board is also a great board for spelling. Prepare three sets of cards with problems of increasing difficulty. Let players choose to try for ten, twenty, or thirty yards. Players begin with their markers at the fifty-yard line.

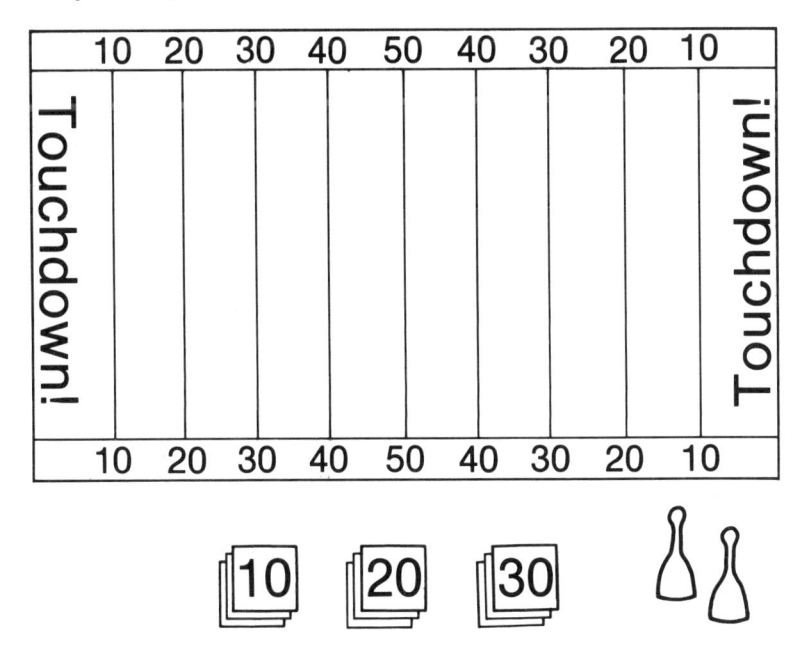

Spelling Races

Spelling is particularly easy to adapt to a board game. Words that frequently pop up misspelled in compositions are:

Contracted words
Animal names
Holiday words
Color words
Number words
Geography terms
Foods
Calendar words
Homonyms

For the homonym group, it is important to print right on the card a clear example of how the word is used. Sentences should be fun, but simple to read, so as not to confuse the speller. Some examples:

1. Peace—Let's have some *peace* and quiet.
2. Piece—I'd like a third *piece* of pie, please.
3. Tail—A squirrel has a bushy *tail*.
4. Tale—Tell me another fairy *tale*.
5. Here—*Here* is the pizza you ordered.
6. Hear—I can *hear* you whispering.
7. Threw—He *threw* a tomato at me.
8. Through—I'm *through* with you.
9. Mail—Put the *mail* in the mailbox.
10. Male—Tom cat means *male* cat.
11. Blue—Violets aren't really *blue,* they're purple.
12. Blew—A gust of wind *blew* my wig off.
13. One—*One* of us is taller.
14. Won—I *won* a trip to Hawaii.
15. Knight—He's a *knight* in shining armor.
16. Night—It rained all *night*.
17. Bare—Trees are *bare* in winter.
18. Bear—A *bear* ate my homework.
19. I—*I* like school.
20. Eye—A Cyclops has one *eye*.
21. By—Let's go *by* the park.
22. Buy—I'd like to *buy* a new bike.
23. Write—Please *write* me a long letter.
24. Right—I'm wrong. You're *right!*
25. Pair—Dorothy had a *pair* of red shoes.
26. Pear—I ate a *pear* for lunch.
27. Cent—I don't have one *cent* left.
28. Sent—I *sent* you a postcard.
29. Scent—A skunk has a strong *scent*.
30. Dear—You are a *dear* child.
31. Deer—We saw three *deer* in the woods.
32. Four—The *four* of us went to lunch.
33. For—I'm looking *for* you.
34. Know—I *know* the answer.
35. No—She won't take *no* for an answer.
36. Nose—My *nose* is cold.
37. Knows—Who *knows* how to play tag?
38. New—I want a *new* pony.

39. Knew—I *knew* you would help me.
40. Break—Give me a *break!*
41. Brake—Slow down. Step on the *brake.*
42. Dew—*Dew* on the grass makes your shoes wet.
43. Do—*Do* you want to go to the movies.
44. Sea—A whale lives in the *sea.*
45. See—I *see* your face.
46. Pail—Bring a *pail* of sand.
47. Pale—Give her a *pale* pink rose.
48. Sale—I got this at a garage *sale.*
49. Sail—Let's *sail* around the world.
50. Ate—She *ate* too much ice cream.
51. Eight—A spider has *eight* legs.

Vocabulary Game Board

This "disposable" game board can serve as an aid to reinforcing vocabulary words for the beginning reader or reviewing definitions for the older reader. Use a piece of colored construction paper and a marker to make this simple game. Younger students can simply read the words, while older students can look up the definitions of vocabulary words on the board.

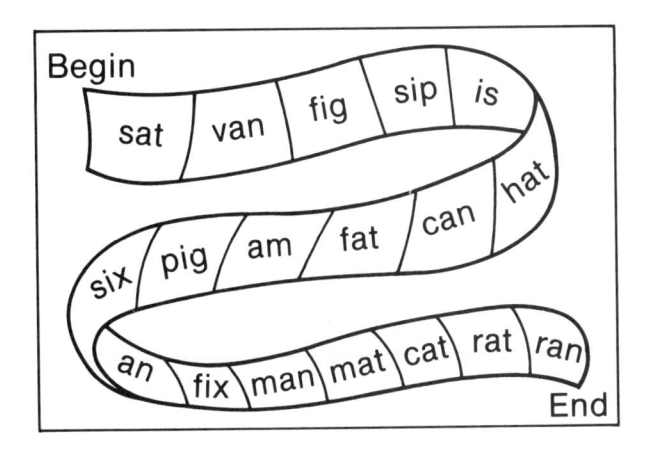

Concentration

This is a popular game for helping beginning readers learn vocabulary words.

Making the game

Make any even number of cards, usually about twenty. Print each word or fact on two cards.

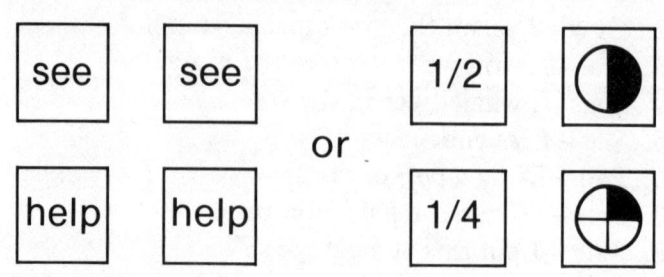

| see | see | | 1/2 | ◐ |

or

| help | help | | 1/4 | ⊕ |

Playing the game

All cards are placed face down in even rows.

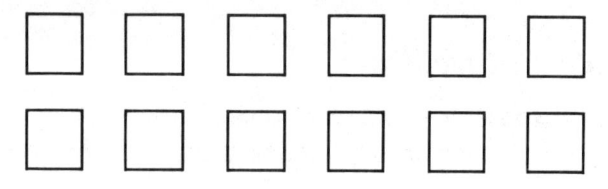

Players take turns flipping over two cards at a time to see if they can find a pair. In a reading game, players must also be able to read the words in order to collect the pair. When a player finds a pair, that player collects the pair and gets to go again. If the two cards do not make a pair, the player turns them face down again. Play continues until all cards are collected. The player with the most cards is the winner.

Uses

Cards can be made for:

Clocks and times
Vocabulary words
States and capitals
Major cities and states
Rivers and countries
Fractions and representations
Decimals and percents
Consonant sounds and pictures
Vowel sounds and pictures
Contractions and separate words
Addition problems and answers
Subtraction problems and answers

Multiplication and division facts
Science terms and definitions
Synonyms
Antonyms
Homonyms
Titles and authors

Note: These cards can also be used to play Go Fish.

Compound Words

Compound words can be learned through several game formats (for example, Go Fish, cover boards, Dominoes), but they are probably easiest for students to understand and work with in the Concentration game format.

Having students form compound words is an excellent way to help them learn to decode these words more easily when they are reading. The manipulation of word parts also helps students to spell compound words.

Since many of the words on the following list can be put together in more than one way, it is a good idea to limit the number of words used for beginning readers. Older students will be able to deal with more word cards and possible combinations.

Compound Word List

some	light	care	place
good	walk	less	up
every	one	where	road
mail	bath	back	stairs
rail	boat	ground	room
not	house	hay	break
day	birth	stack	fast
table	bird	any	foot
door	side	man	ball
in	wind	cloth	ward
fire	can	bell	straw
be	mill	self	berry
board	out	thing	down
card	bed	bye	town
ways	wheel	him	sail
camp	chair		

Time, Please

Parents and teachers frequently lament, "Kids can't learn to tell time with all these digital clocks around." No doubt about it, digital clocks are here to stay. But we've always had a variety of clocks, from cuckoo clocks to tiny watches without any numbers at all. This Concentration format game takes into account some of the variations in time telling. Here are some cards for a game of Time, Please:

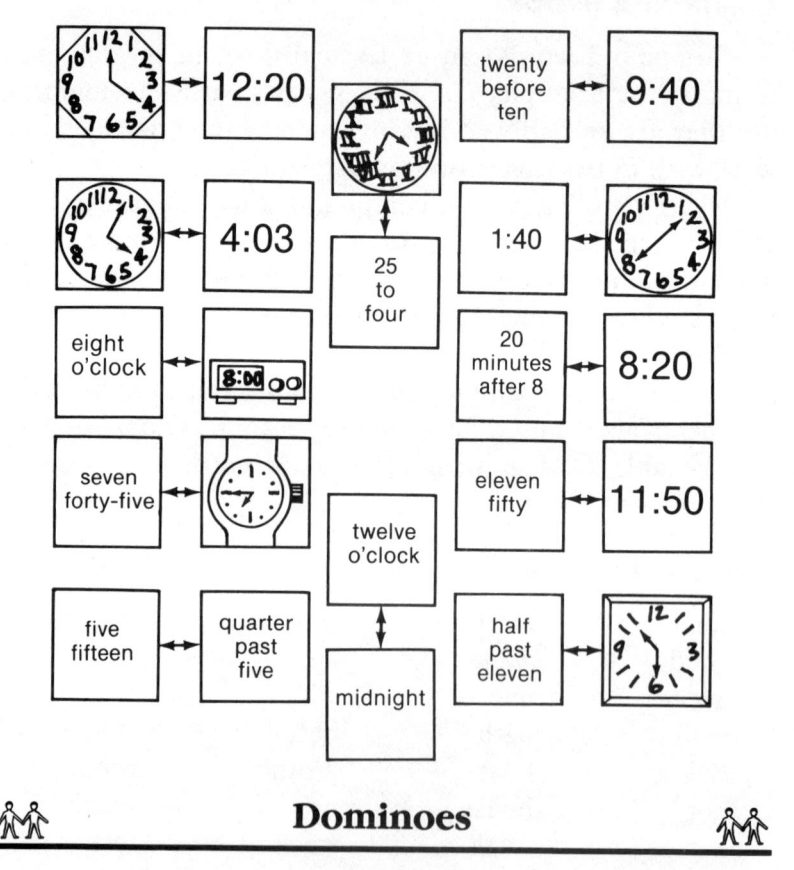

Dominoes

This is a simplified version of the standard Dominoes game. It can be made simple, to help children learn basic skills, or more challenging.

Making the game

Begin by making lists of math facts or phonics sounds to be used. Make twenty to forty cards, and use each fact or sound three or four times. The cards have two sections each, and the game is played by matching like facts.

For example:

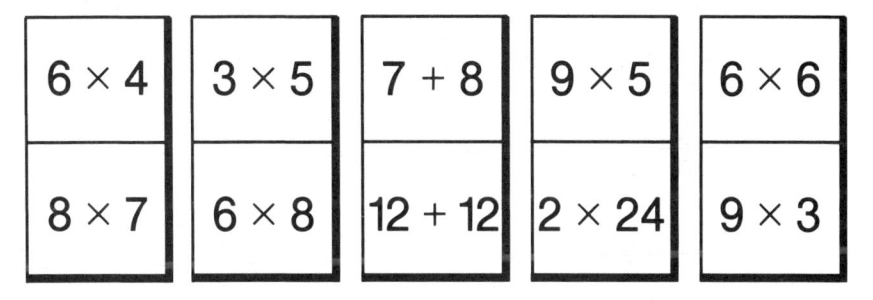

6 × 4	3 × 5	7 + 8	9 × 5	6 × 6
8 × 7	6 × 8	12 + 12	2 × 24	9 × 3

Playing the game

Competitive Version: Set one card face up in the middle of the playing area. Give each player five cards. The players take turns adding cards to the cards in the middle. Cards can be attached anywhere, in any direction, as long as touching sections match. If a player has no card to add, he or she draws from a pile of cards turned face down. The game ends when one player uses up all of his or her cards.

Cooperative Version: Set one card face up in the middle of the playing area. Divide the remainder equally among the players. Everyone plays at once. This method works best when the game is difficult. The object is to use up the entire deck. Players who finish first help the remaining players.

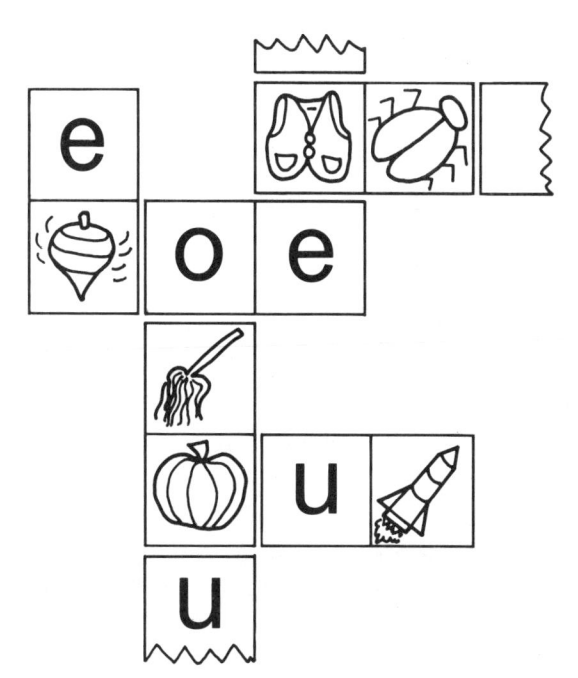

33

Rhyming Dominoes

Reading and hearing rhyming words gives young readers practice with phonetic concepts and accurate pronunciation.

Rhyming words for beginning readers:

    drink - sink - think - pink
    bill - dill - grill - will - hill
    fan - can - pan
    sail - bale - pail
    led - said - red - bed
    tune - spoon - soon - moon
    wrote - float - coat - boat
    day - play - lay - say - gray
    flat - hat - that - mat - cat

Rhyming words for middle grade children:

    comb - foam - home - chrome - tome
    catch - latch - scratch - detach
    blade - braid - they'd - maid - afraid
    bear - care - chair - fair - there - glare
    ate - bait - weight - straight - crate
    break - ache - shake - steak - opaque
    ham - lamb - jamb - swam
    steam - theme - scream - teem - beam
    freak - leek - unique - weak - Greek
    earth - mirth - berth - worth
    meat - fleet - petite - repeat - obsolete
    chime - climb - rhyme - grime - mime

Rhyming words for advanced readers:

    waif - safe - chafe
    giraffe - carafe - behalf - graph
    nomad - plaid - Olympiad - lad - clad
    ere - heir - compare - prayer - despair
    fault - vault - malt - assault - exalt
    bazaar - caviar - czar - are - guitar
    niece - obese - fleece - police - cease
    pique - antique - meek - wreak - sheik - chic
    skis - appease - seize - chemise - trapeze
    lieu - cue - revenue - adieu - stew - curfew - view

choir - mire - spire - pyre - lyre - sapphire
cajole - soul - droll - mole - bowl - parole

Consult a rhyming dictionary for additional words.

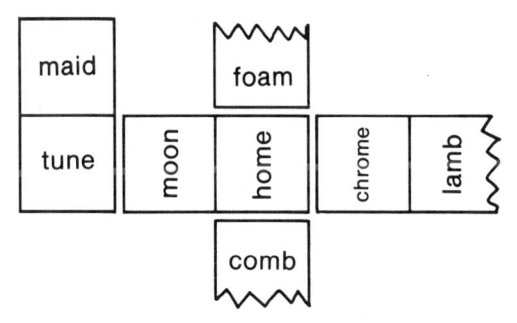

```
         ┌──────┐
         │ foam │
┌──────┐ │      │ ┌──────┐
│ maid │ ├──────┤ │      │
│      │ │ moon │ │      │
├──────┤ │ home │ │      │
│ tune │ │      │ │chrome│
│      │ │      │ │ lamb │
└──────┘ ├──────┤ └──────┘
         │ comb │
         │      │
         └──────┘
```

Phonics Dominoes

Phonics Dominoes is a good game for demonstrating that some letters have many sounds, and various letter combinations sometimes have the same sound. This confusing concept can be sorted out graphically in a game of Phonics Dominoes.

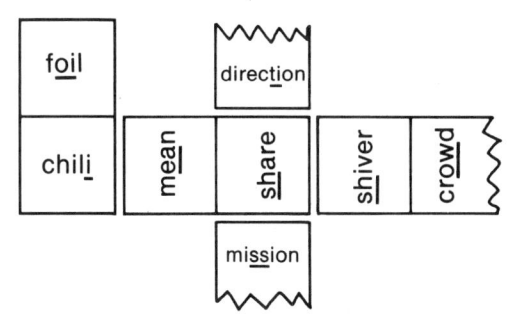

```
         ┌────────┐
         │direction│
┌──────┐ │        │ ┌──────┐
│ foil │ ├────────┤ │      │
│      │ │ mean   │ │shiver│
├──────┤ │ share  │ │crowd │
│ chili│ │        │ │      │
│      │ ├────────┤ └──────┘
└──────┘ │mission │
         └────────┘
```

Sample words for Phonics Dominoes:

bright - kite - lye - fry

telegraph - reef - fiddle - enough

mission - share - shiver - direction

giraffe - gentle - jiggle - range

myth - middle - wrist

sentence - moss - celery - face

blue - moon - move - blew - shoe - tube - boot - two - school

blow - rose

m__ean - ch__ili - p__eel - fr__eeze - __even - h__eat

l__etter - bu__tter - wh__irl - col__or - n__urse

m__end - h__ead - inst__ead - sl__ed

n__oise - f__oil - t__oys

tod__ay - s__ail - cl__ay - sn__ail - p__aid

cr__owd - sh__out - f__ound

dr__aw - h__all - w__ant

Go Fish

This well-loved children's game can be used to teach nearly all basic skills. It is especially good for reviewing vocabulary with beginning readers.

Making the game
 Make twenty to forty game cards in pairs. The cards may have matching words, math facts, or other items.

Playing the game
 The cards are shuffled and each player is dealt five cards. The remaining cards are placed in a pile face down. Players take turns asking any other player for a specific card in order to make a pair.

If the player being asked does not have that card, he says, "Go fish," and the asking player draws a card from the pile. Any time the player gets his card from another player or from the pile, he gets to ask again.

Whenever a player has a matched set in his hand, he or she lays it down, face up. The game is over when one player is out of cards.

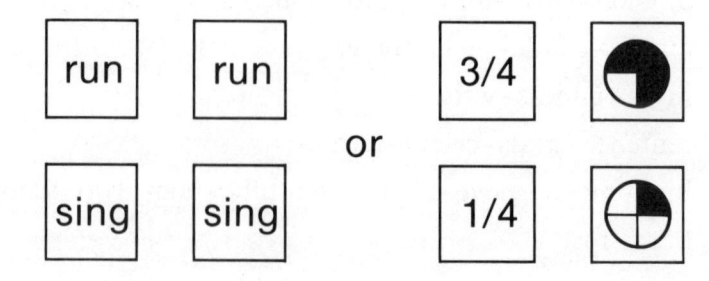

Fractions, Percents, and Decimals

Go Fish can be played just as easily with sets of three cards instead of pairs.

This game is designed for children in the upper grades who are studying the relationship between fractions, percents, and decimals. Memorizing a few common sets will be helpful in a number of situations. These numerical expressions are commonly used in reading materials, on television, in radio news reports, in advertising, and in math and science studies. This game can also be played in pocket puzzle format.

Make cards with the following numerical expressions.

Percent	*Decimal*	*Fraction*
100%	1.0	1/1
90%	.9	9/10
80%	.8	4/5
75%	.75	3/4
66%	.66	2/3
60%	.6	3/5
50%	.5	1/2
40%	.4	2/5
33%	.33	1/3
25%	.25	1/4
10%	.1	1/10
1%	.01	1/100

Turnover Games

This variation of a board game allows children to practice relatively new material because it helps them learn the correct answers.

Making the game

Make a set of cards with questions or problems on one side and answers on the other.

Playing the game

Players lay out the cards on a table or floor, question sides facing up. The cards should form a linear pattern with clear start and finish points. Each card counts as one space. A player rolls the die or dice and moves a marker the correct number of spaces. The player then answers the question and turns the card over to check the answer. If correct, the player stays; if incorrect, the player returns to his or her former position.

The game ends when one or both players have reached the finish point.

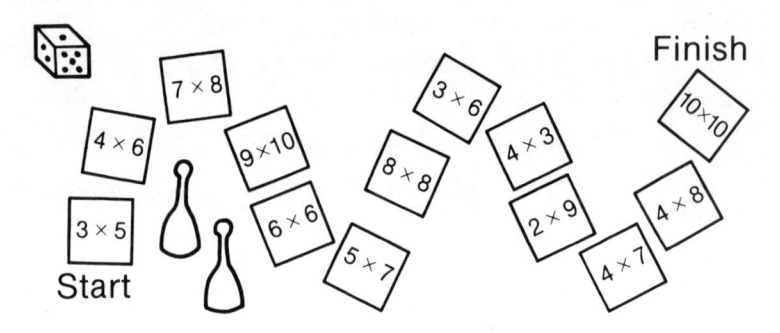

What Time Is It?

Time-telling skills are reinforced easily in a turnover game.

Draw or stamp clock faces on twenty-four cards. Draw hands to indicate hour and half-hour times. On the backs of the cards, write the corresponding time for each clock.

To play the game, students lay the cards out in a turnover game format.

Each player shakes the die, moves ahead the number of spaces indicated, and gives the time for that clock. The player checks the answer on the back. If correct, the player stays; if incorrect, the player returns to his or her former position.

For more advanced time telling skills, draw the hands to indicate times at five-minute or one-minute intervals.

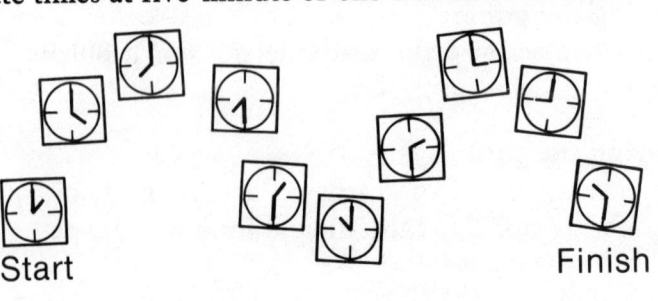

Money, Money, Money

Most students are eager to learn to count money. An inexpensive box of play money with coins included can be used to make cards with varying amounts of dollars and cents. This turnover game can be made for several levels of ability: small coins and one and five dollar bills for second grade students, and unlimited combinations for third grade and older students.

Simply cut the edges of the bills off and glue them on cards along with some cardboard coins. These cards will need to be laminated or covered with clear contact paper. Write the amount shown in bills and coins on the back of the card.

War

War can be used for reviewing and practicing all kinds of basic math facts.

Making the game

Cards for War are simply cards with numerals on them. Make about fifty or sixty cards. Regular playing cards can be used for some games. Because playing cards have both numbers and figures that represent the numbers (five hearts and a number 5, for example), players will be able to count the figures instead of adding. These cards can be used to acquaint very young players with addition facts. Tip: The ink from permanent markers often shows through on index cards. Watercolor markers are less likely to cause this problem.

Playing the Game

Divide the deck equally between two players. They place their cards face down in a stack. Each player turns up two cards and adds (or subtracts or multiplies) the two numbers.

The player with the highest total takes all four cards and places them face down on the bottom of his stack. If a player catches his opponent in a calculation error, he gets to collect all four cards regardless of whose total is higher.

If the totals are equal, players turn up two more cards and add (subtract or multiply) them. The player with the highest total takes all eight cards.

Variations

The player with the lowest rather than the highest total can collect the cards.

To practice adding columns and adding large numbers, players can lay out three or four cards at a time. The play continues until one player runs out of cards.

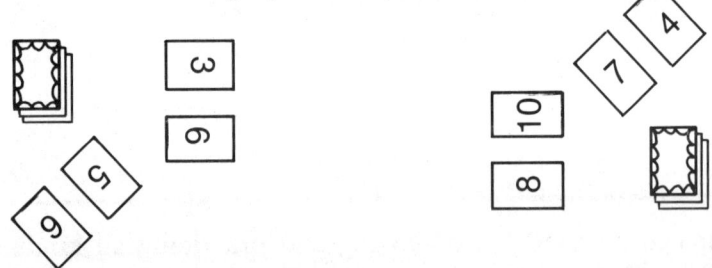

Pocket Puzzles and Cover Boards

These activities are games for one person. They are useful for a variety of reasons. You may want to use them to:

- give to a student who prefers to work alone.
- make a specific assignment for a student.
- check a student's knowledge or skill in a nonthreatening way.

Pocket puzzles and cover boards are used by most kindergarten teachers, but their use can be expanded to the middle and upper grades. Prefixes, suffixes, multiplication facts, fractions, consonant sounds, and counting activities may be used in this format as well. Older students will enjoy the variety these puzzles provide. Some examples of pocket puzzles and cover boards are described below.

Short Vowels Pocket Puzzle

Provide twenty to thirty pictures of short vowel words to be inserted into the appropriate pockets.

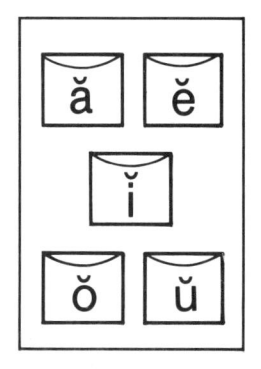

Short and Long Vowels Pocket Puzzle

Provide thirty to forty word or picture cards with long and short vowel sounds. Mark pockets with short and long vowels.

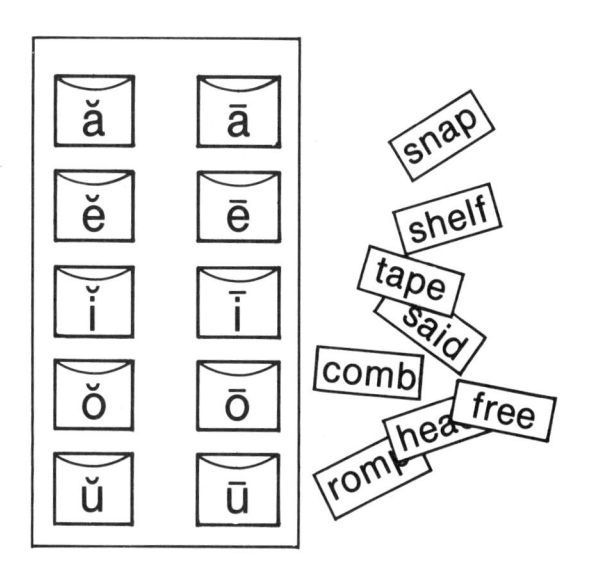

Math Facts Cover Board

Mark cookie jar shapes with math problems. Cut out lids and mark them with the answers. Students must cover each cookie jar shape with the correct lid.

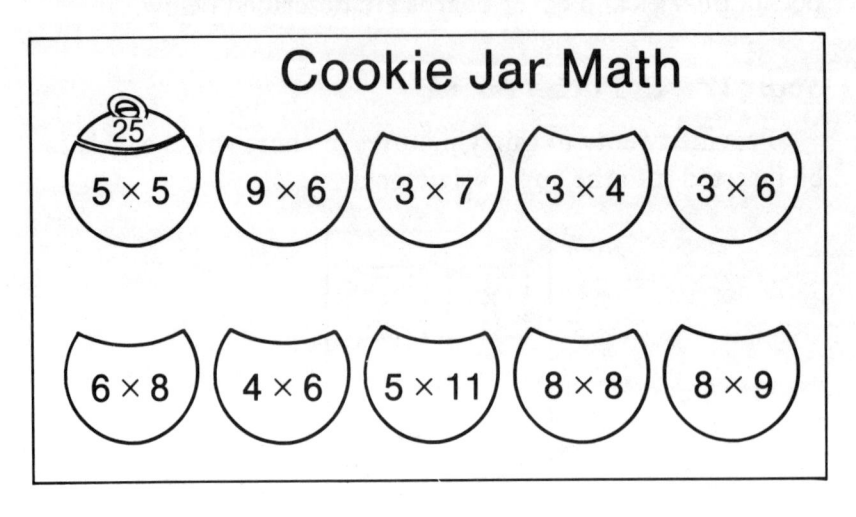

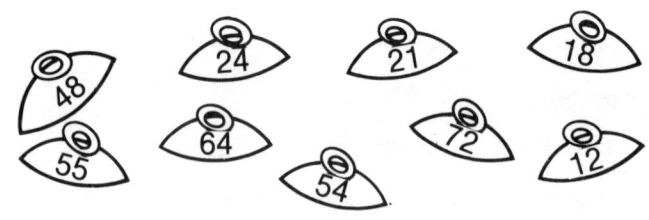

Cookie Jar Math

- 25
- 5 × 5
- 9 × 6
- 3 × 7
- 3 × 4
- 3 × 6
- 6 × 8
- 4 × 6
- 5 × 11
- 8 × 8
- 8 × 9

Lids: 48, 24, 21, 18, 55, 64, 54, 72, 12

Contractions Cover Board

Mark wagon shapes with contractions. Write the words that form the contractions on separate wheel shapes. Ask students to add the wheels to the wagons.

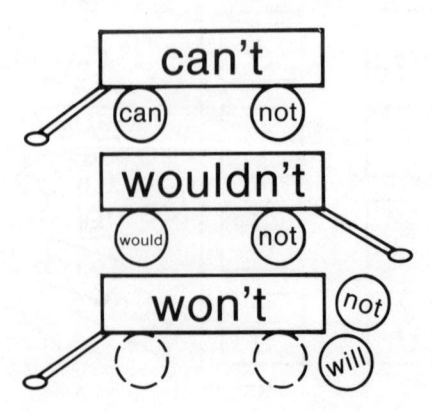

- can't — (can) (not)
- wouldn't — (would) (not)
- won't — (not) (will)

42

Other Games

The games and activities in this section vary in format somewhat from the basic seven games, yet they are still skill intensive, easy to make, and easy to play.

Read and Answer

This is a favorite game of students of many ages. The list of questions presented here is geared to readers at approximately second grade level. Teachers can prepare their own cards to reflect any level of reading and any type of factual recall they desire.

Making the game

The materials for this game consist only of a stack of 3" × 5" index cards with questions printed on them.

Playing the game

Cards are placed face down on a table or floor and students take turns reading them. The questions are written so that if a student can read the card, he or she can most likely answer the question. When the student is unable to decipher the key words in the question, it will be difficult to understand and respond appropriately. If a student reads the question and gives an answer that is satisfactory to teammates, the student keeps the card. Teammates may check the card to see if it was read correctly. If the card is read incorrectly or the player is unable to answer the question, the card goes to the bottom of the pile. This is a good game for three or four players.

Sample questions
- For what do you use scissors?
- Name a state in the western (southern) (eastern) region of the United States.
- How many people are there in your family?
- What is a typhoon? (hurricane?) (tornado?)
- When during the day is your shadow the shortest?
- What ocean is near California? (New York?)
- What is produced on a dairy farm?
- What is a fossil?

- How many planets are there in our solar system?
- What are two animals that lay eggs?
- Which group of animals is coldblooded?
- What is the speed limit on our highways?
- Name the secondary colors.
- What is the longest journey you have ever taken?
- Rhode Island is the smallest state in our country. Name another small state.
- Which is larger: a giraffe or a gerbil?
- Name the four food groups.
- How many states are in the United States?
- Name a food you like to eat.
- Name a good activity for a Saturday afternoon.
- How can you avoid spreading germs when you have a cold?
- In what state do you live?
- Name three types of food you might put in a sandwich.
- How old will you be in the year 2000?
- What two colors do you combine to make green?
- Name two things you might see at an airport.
- What number comes after ninety-nine?
- Which is stronger: an elephant or an egret?
- Who takes the attendance at school?
- Geography is the study of what?
- What color are your eyes?
- Where do you sit when you watch television?
- About how much do you weigh?
- Where does wool come from?
- What month comes after January?
- What town (city) do you live in or near?
- Name three mammals.
- Who are your neighbors?
- What animal has a trunk?
- What would you say if you hit your finger with a hammer?
- How old are you?
- Say two words that rhyme.
- Name the primary colors.
- What does it mean to be excited? (dejected?) (exuberant?)
- Do you like basketball, football, baseball, or soccer best?
- What might make an ice cube disappear?

- Name something you do during recess.
- During what season of the year would you make a snowman?
- Name three animals you might find in the jungle.
- How many months are there in a year?
- How many days are there in a week?
- What is your favorite movie?
- Name three things that use electricity to run.
- How many children are there in our school?
- What do you add to three to make five?
- What animal has a pouch to carry its babies?
- What school subject do you like best?
- What are windows made of?
- Name something you might wear on your wrist.
- Which day comes after Sunday?
- Name three continents.
- Name a mammal that lives in the water.
- Who comes down the chimney at Christmas?
- Who was our first President?
- What are two ingredients in ice cream?

Globe Trotting

This geography game provides students with practice in reading the names of countries and using a globe to check their geography knowledge.

The cards include the names of countries as well as the following types of questions:

- Name a country on the equator.
- Name a country north of Spain (Zimbabwe) (India).
- Name a country in Asia (Europe) (North America).
- Name a country north (south) of the equator.
- Name a river in Europe (North America) (Asia) (South America).

Making the game

To play this geography game, students need a game board, a die or dice, a globe, a cloth to cover the globe, and cards with appropriate geography questions. Some cards may have the name of a country.

Playing the game

The player throws a die and picks up a card. If the player draws the name of a country, he or she tells which continent that country is a part of. If one of the other short answer cards is drawn, the player answers accordingly. The other player then uncovers the globe to check the answer. If the answer is correct, the player moves his or her marker the number of spaces indicated by the die. If the answer is incorrect, the other player draws a card.

This game may move along a little more slowly than some, but helping students become familiar with the globe is well worth the time.

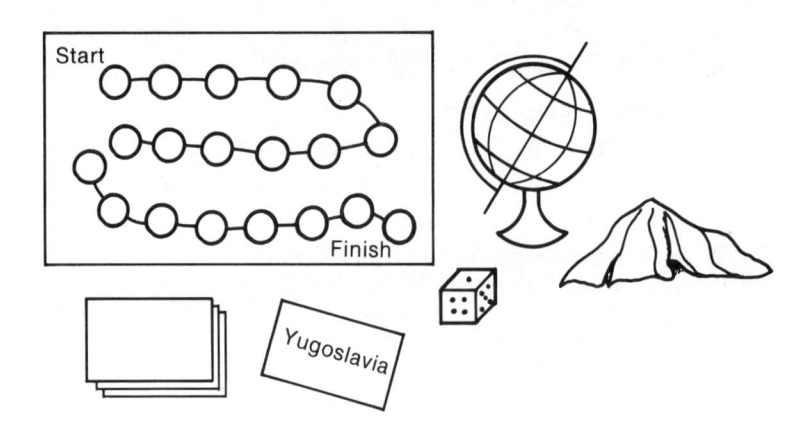

Inchworm and Centimeter Snake

Both of these board games are constructed with the same design. The difference between them is the measurement lines located in the upper righthand corner. Both games give students practice in measuring. Their primary use is in kindergarten and first grade and again in the upper grades, when students are learning to measure fractions of an inch and measure to the nearest 1/8", 1/16", and so on.

Cards have the letters *A* to *H* printed on the back. To play Inchworm, each player draws a card, measures the line segment indicated by the letter on the card, and moves a corresponding number of spaces. If line *A*, for example, is five inches long, the student would move five spaces. To play Centimeter Snake, students measure with a centimeter ruler.

For older students learning fractional measurements, numerators of fractions can be used to indicate the number of spaces to move. For example, 1-7/8" equals seven spaces, 2-3/4" equals three spaces. The game is over when one player reaches the tail of the snake or worm.

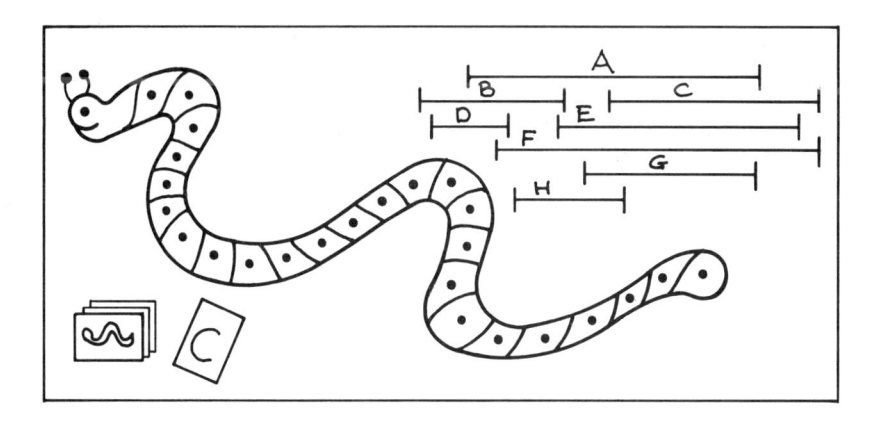

Chapter 4

Setting Up a Reading Program

For beginning readers, the most important element in any reading program is the opportunity to read aloud. Studying phonics, comprehension, vocabulary building, and other related tasks are important, but oral reading is essential. Most of the words that children learn to read in the first few years of schooling are already familiar to them. The student's task is to begin to recognize these familiar words in their printed forms. To oversimplify a bit, this is a process of matching. The student must match printed words to spoken words. The use of pictures may be helpful, but the best way to improve one's reading skills at this stage is to read aloud to someone who can catch and correct errors.

Virtually every person who has ever attended an American elementary school can recall the reading circles. The class is divided into groups and the teacher has a time period during which each group reads with him or her. Because a reading group may consist of six or more students and may spend about half an hour with the teacher, a student has no more than five minutes of oral reading practice during such a session, if, in fact, *all* of that time is spent reading. Usually there is some discussion, some lecturing, and some wasted time. In many situations the teacher is not able to meet with every group every day; this may mean that a student's opportunity to practice reading aloud could total as little as fifteen minutes per week.

If the teacher is willing to use students as tutors, however, each student could easily read aloud for ten to fifteen minutes each day. The only prerequisite a reading tutor must meet is that he or she must be able to read the material that another student will be reading to him or her. Two students may be able to read to the same tutor at once, but three are probably too many. The objective is to provide the maximum opportunity for actual reading.

It takes a bit of engineering to devise a system that pairs each student with a tutor (see Chapter 2), but it is well worth the effort. In the case of the highest-level readers in the class, the teacher may have to bring in tutors from another class. This should not be too difficult; most schools and teachers are favorably disposed toward cross-age tutoring, and students usually jump at the chance to have such a special assignment.

For the youngest students (preprimer and primer level), it is helpful to have vocabulary cards prepared. These can be standard flashcards or game cards for Go Fish or Concentration. An effective assignment pattern for this level is to read yesterday's story, plus one new story, and then have students use the flashcards or play with the game cards.

Older students (first primer and above) can simply read a new story or section each day. The repetition and review at this level is built in because each story contains many of the same words. If there are questions at the end of the story, the tutor and the student can read and answer them orally. If you prefer, the student can write out the answers independently. Having had the oral review, the student should be able to complete the assignment more accurately.

Students in the upper elementary grades who read independently can be paired together for oral reading practice. Students at fourth, fifth, or sixth grade reading levels are no longer completely dependent on oral practice to advance their reading skills. They can use context clues or look up words in glossaries and dictionaries; in other words, these students are beginning to *use* their reading skills to *improve* their reading.

Actual experience and specific skills may vary widely even between two students whose graded reading levels are similar. What this means for peer teaching is that these older students can read aloud to each other, each student acting as both tutor and student. There is a good chance that a word or meaning unknown to one of them will be familiar to the other. If they are both stumped, they can ask another student, jot the word down and check it later, consult the teacher, or use any other means which has been outlined for them by the teacher.

Sessions for reading aloud can be scheduled throughout the morning to prevent the classroom from becoming overly noisy. A staggered schedule will happen as a matter of course if students are permitted to organize their own morning work schedules. The tutor should be the one to pick the time to read and gather the students and materials together.

Keep students and tutors together in the same groups or pairs for as long as possible. A number of circumstances will necessitate change; some students will move away, someone may progress rapidly and outgrow his or her tutor, and some students will not work well together. Yet most students will develop a good working relationship. In forming the initial groups or pairs, you might ask students whom they would like to work with. This input helps prevent changes in student-tutor assignments later on. It has been my experience that students who are friends work very well together; they feel motivated to help each other learn and make good progress.

When students are reading to each other, you can do two things:

1. Listen to students whose tutors are absent.
2. Walk around the room and listen to students and tutors, giving help to tutors about what to correct and how.

One of the least obtrusive ways you can point out an error is to simply point to the word that was mispronounced or skipped with the eraser end of a pencil, without saying anything. If the student cannot correct the error after one try, the tutor can say the word correctly and the reader can move on. By assisting the tutor rather than helping the student directly, you can avoid usurping the tutor's role. A tutor who is paying close attention to the student is also reading. He or she is probably reading more carefully than usual because the job of tutoring requires it. This, of course, means that the tutor is getting a reading lesson also.

Allowing the readers to move about and get set up on an independent schedule gives you greater flexibility in monitoring and teaching oral reading. It is easier and faster to move yourself about the room than to collect an entire group of readers together. When you stand or sit beside a tutor/reader pair for a few minutes and all is moving smoothly, you can simply move away without disturbing the team and go listen to someone else. In this manner, you can move about the room, stopping to give instruction and hints where needed, and leave alone those students who are managing effectively on their own. Students, of course, are free to call on you when they want assistance.

The conscientious teacher is now asking, "But when do I teach reading?" The answer: "All day long." When you answer a question, supply a word, explain a concept, demonstrate a phonics rule, or give an example, you are teaching reading. Although teaching to large groups may seem to be an efficient use of time, it is not necessarily an efficient way for students to learn. A student is most receptive to a bit of information at the precise time a question has formed in his or her mind about that item, topic, or concept.

Teaching word recognition is greatly enhanced by the use of a superior phonics workbook, one that students can work through at their own pace. In this way, each student is presented with word study concepts at a rate at which he or she can absorb and comprehend them. When a student comes to a concept that demands more explanation than the book provides, he or she can seek out the teacher or a student tutor for a private two- or three-minute lesson.

When Malcolm brings his phonics book to the teacher's desk to ask about adding "ing" endings and doubling consonants, and the teacher discusses this with him, writes out a few examples on scratch paper, and has him answer a few questions, he will remember and understand virtually everything that was discussed. He had the opportunity to ask questions immediately if he did not understand what was being explained. In listening to the same subject discussed in a large group, Malcolm may not have been in the least interested because he hadn't come to "that page" yet. He may have been preoccupied with counting the beads in a little girl's hair ties, watching the teacher's shirtsleeves or ruffles jiggle while he or she wrote on the chalkboard, or his question may have been met with, "Just a minute, Malcolm."

It is helpful for you to sit with a group of students occasionally and practice or review some kinds of skills, but it is probably not in the best interest of the students to *rely* on this type of teaching. Use group instruction after students have demonstrated a common need for similar information or help. If, for instance, several students within the space of two or three days have had difficulty finding root words or using semicolons, you can gather those students together and conduct a lesson. You may present a similar lesson to a different group of students at a later date. Each presentation should be given in response to the students' needs. By teaching in this way, you also avoid placing the students in permanent groups for instruction, groups which usually become stigmatized as high or low, fast or slow, and so on. Instructional groups are functional, flexible, and temporary.

Many teachers may have a greater need for permanent procedures, groups, and systems than this method provides. One of the most frequently given reasons for using systematic approaches in classroom instruction is that "the children need the stability of a schedule and a routine." It's true that many children become upset when their daily classroom routine is changed. The cause for such a response, however, is debatable. If teachers go to such great lengths to establish permanent order for every aspect of classroom life, it is no wonder that children become accustomed to routine. Whether routine is an innate need of youngsters that teachers respond to, or whether teaching is a profession that attracts people who prefer routines, is open to question.

In his landmark book *Democracy and Education*, John Dewey wrote, "All communication is like art. It may be fairly said, therefore, that any social arrangement that remains vitally shared, is educative to those who participate in it. Only when it becomes cast in a mold and runs in a routine does it lose its educative power." By and large, children and adults function well when expectations are clearly stated, responses are immediate and mostly positive, and flexibility is the rule rather than the exception.

Chapter 5
Motivation and Discipline

When you decide to encourage students to help each other and to take some responsibility for the success of their peers, you are doing more than finding an efficient way to teach. In all likelihood, to make peer teaching work effectively, you will need to examine some of the implicit messages in employing such strategies. Peer teaching alters your role in the classroom, changes your relationship with the students, and changes the students' relationships with each other. Such a dramatic revision of roles calls for, at least, a review of methods and strategies which conventionally fall into the realm of discipline. The following ideas and suggestions will help you create an atmosphere conducive to successful peer teaching.

Motivation and discipline are dealt with here as two sides of the same coin. Classroom discipline is generally thought of as a collection of philosophies and techniques applied by a teacher to check counterproductive behaviors. Motivation is usually defined as the collection of philosophies and techniques used by a teacher to inspire students to perform well, both socially and academically. To "check," in this instance, suggests to hold back, to control, or to stop. These meanings seem to be in diametric opposition to the term "inspire," which might be thought of as a means of bringing forth, promoting, or energizing. How are these seeming opposites related? Many educational theorists and psychologists—Jerome Bruner, Carl Rogers, Jean Piaget, Maria Montessori, and John Holt among them—have postulated that motivation comes from within. The challenge presented by these noted educators and authors is for parents and teachers to keep motivation high and curiosity alive while instilling in the child a sense of discipline and promoting socially acceptable behavior.

Most of the currently popular techniques for classroom discipline emphasize that teachers clearly define unacceptable behaviors and explain their consequences. Many of these techniques employ the principles of behavior modification. The systematic aspect of such approaches is often what appeals to classroom teachers. A clearly defined system of rules fits well with the demands for accountability and fairness which are part of the business of education today. School rules, like state and federal laws, represent a list of what not to do, with stated consequences for unacceptable behavior.

Jerome Bruner noted in his book, *On Knowing: Essays for the Left Hand*, "Our insights into mental functioning are too often fashioned from observations of the sick and the handicapped. It is difficult to catch and record, no less to understand, the swift flight of man's mind operating at its best." I believe we fall prey to a similar phenomenon in the classroom. Teachers often base their rules for conduct on the behaviors which cause the most disturbance in the classroom. The discussion below outlines a strategy for teaching discipline almost as if it were a subject. This approach appeals to the students' intellect and helps them develop standards for behavior.

I suggest that teachers present their students with a description of valuable human qualities. The means for the presentation depends on the teacher's wishes and the students' age, maturity, and background. Younger students rely more heavily on oral communication and dramatic presentations to derive the meaning of a concept. With older students, written communication and allegory help to convey the message.

There is no standardized list of desirable qualities, but such a list might include fairness, responsibility, consideration, trustworthiness, kindness, dependability, courtesy, honesty, tolerance, sportsmanship, and cooperation. All persons wish to be treated courteously, fairly, and with kindness. It is easy to illustrate to students of any age the advantages of these virtues. The kinds of traits one includes on such a list are those that are universally respected. Compliance and obedience are convenient childhood traits, but in many situations compliance would be self-destructive adult behavior. Cooperation, on the other hand, is a related virtue, and it is a valuable trait in both youth and adulthood.

By outlining what kinds of behavior and attitudes are desirable, you can make a strong statement about the goals you have for students in terms of both classroom interaction and individual welfare. This attention to standards is like a syllabus for personal growth. Your presentation should convey that "good" behavior is not simply a matter of obeying rules. Good behavior is a result of either a conscious decision to act in a particular way or a matter of an automatic response. In the latter case, good behavior occurs if the child has a repertoire of automatic behaviors that are considered pleasant and constructive; these, of course, are influenced by the child's temperament and background.

Intervention on the part of an adult usually takes place when:

1. a child decides to do something he should not do.
2. a child gets into a situation where he or she does not understand the implications of certain behaviors.
3. a child does not possess the automatic responses which are socially acceptable.

Depending on the particular circumstances, the adult:

1. intervenes immediately and forcefully (this does not imply physical force).
2. gets the child's attention and conveys a brief message.
3. makes a mental note to take care of the problem at a later time.

In all these situations, an "educational" approach can be of help. Goal-oriented activities and discussions help to bring automatic or habitual behaviors into conscious thought. Having preset standards of behavior will aid you in each situation. These standards give you a point of reference for communicating with students in a constructive way.

For example, to intervene immediately and forcefully, a teacher might say, "Ben, please stand outside the door. You may return when you are able to show more consideration for your classmates."

To get a child's attention and convey a brief message, a teacher might say, "Lillian, I would like you to think of a more courteous way to say that."

A teacher may also deal with problem behaviors at a later time. For instance, "Boys and girls, I noticed this morning on the playground that there were children calling out insults during a game of soccer. Good sportsmanship means shouting encouragement to other players. Perhaps we can come up with some slogans to call out for different kinds of plays."

In all three instances the prior groundwork laid down through class discussions of desired behavior serves as a reference for both the students and the teacher. The teacher is able to point out the need for improved conduct and call upon the students to make a move toward that conduct. The teacher moves quickly away from the problem toward a solution that involves the students.

In *Democracy and Education,* John Dewey wrote, "When we confuse a physical with an educative result, we always lose the chance of enlisting the person's own participation in getting the result desired and thereby of developing within him an intrinsic and persisting direction in the right way." This idea directly relates to the motivation and discipline proposal in this chapter. It is much easier to get students to move toward something than away from something. Education is not only a matter of getting students to complete assignments and follow rules. There is nothing inherently good about completing tasks and following directions, as history clearly reveals. The value of these things lies in the choices we ultimately make for ourselves about rules, tasks, work, and recreation.

> **Creative Discipline**
> 1. Post a list of universally desirable qualities: cooperation, trustworthiness, kindness, and so on.
> 2. Discuss the meanings of these qualities briefly with students, one term at a time.
> 3. Conduct miniature activities using the terms on your list. These might include compositions, homework, and skits.
> 4. Refer to these qualities when discussing behavior problems with children.
> 5. Have students look for examples of these virtues in various situations.
> 6. Strive to demonstrate these qualities.

It is widely accepted that the most valuable character traits are not learned through instruction, but by example. Children are exposed to many kinds of behavior. Attempts to shelter children and provide only positive examples are frustrating at best. It is the responsibility of adults to help clarify for children the effects of various behaviors and attitudes.

Children frequently have a much wider range of feelings and frustrations than the vocabulary to express these emotions. Feeling impatient, for example, is a common experience for youngsters, but not many children of five, six, or seven years are adept at recognizing and describing impatience in themselves. More importantly, many have not learned to cultivate patience.

When dealing with young children, adults need to explain what patience is, rather than simply respond to acts of jumping, shouting, and fidgeting. Adults know that such actions, in and of themselves, are neither "good" nor "bad" behaviors. But given the many restrictions on certain activities, children probably do think of them in this way. This is not to imply that immediate behavior need not be dealt with; it clearly must. My suggestion is that the child be given a more complete explanation of the desired response than is customary. Helping students develop patience, then, is the ultimate goal. The goal is not to stop children from jumping, but to let them discover their own ways of demonstrating the positive qualities they are forging within.

Whether you use a particular approach to discipline is determined by many different factors. School policies, your own ideology, and individual circumstances are just a few of the elements that come into play when you make decisions about classroom management. But discipline basically consists of personal communication between a teacher and a student. While you may employ a certain system of strategies, the messages the student receives are personal. There is no effective way to depersonalize one-to-one communication. If, as Dewey said, "All communication is like art," then balancing the need for motivation and the need for discipline is also no less than an art.

The underlying principles of this approach to discipline are twofold. First, the approach maximizes student involvement and responsibility. Second, it embraces the concept of movement toward something, which is the essence of motivation. It places a carrot in front of the horse, rather than a bit in its mouth.

If dependence breeds hostility, as suggested by psychologist Haim Ginott, then an approach to discipline which emphasizes discussion and de-emphasizes the teacher's directions will reduce hostility and alleviate tension. The aim of a discussion is that those involved listen, observe, think, and make their own decisions. Yet the response to a teacher's directions can only be compliance or defiance. The independence you give students in a peer teaching program can be enhanced by a form of discipline which also credits them with the ability to make judgments about behavior and interactions, and grants them the opportunity to decide rather than to comply whenever possible.